From Desperation to Dedication: Lessons You Can Bank On

Troy D. Evans

From Desperation to Dedication:
Lessons You Can Bank On

http://www.troyevans.com
2003

From Desperation to Dedication: Lessons You Can Bank On

By

Troy D. Evans

Dedication

To my beautiful wife, Pam - my encourager, my believer, my best friend and my lover- I could not have done this without your support.

To my son, Eric- the one who never stopped believing in me - your belief fueled my desire.

To my parents, Mel and Joyce - you two set the fine example that I would one day discover, and you never gave up on me. Your love and support made me believe in myself.

To my brother and sister, Greg and Kim - you held me closest when I needed you the most. Thank you for the chance to be the big brother I never was.

To my dog, Archibald D. Evans III (Archie) - you sit under my desk all day long, listening to my ramblings - may I someday be the man you think I am!

Contents

Preface:
Panty Hose and a Pistol

*"It is not important how we come to the events in our life.
What is important is how we deal with those events."*

-*Troy Evans*

Pantyhose and a pistol. I am sure that neither the Hanes
Corporation nor Smith & Wesson ever intended for the two
to be used within the same sentence, or as the title of this
book's preface. As a former bank robber, however, these
were the tools of my trade. As a professional speaker, they
continue to be today.

When delivering a presentation on making life changes, I
start by thanking the audience for their time, and letting them
know that it is both my pleasure and my honor to be there
with them to share my story. I then ask them to take a close
look at my face. I explain that this is the face of a loving
husband and father. This is the face of a recent college
graduate who earned both of his degrees with the highest
academic honors. This is the face of a kind man, an honest
man, a trustworthy man and a man of his word. For humor, I
throw in that this just may be the face of a man who could sit
them down at their kitchen table and sell them a term life
insurance policy. As the chuckles die down, I again ask them
to take a close look at this face. I then turn my back to the
audience, pull a pantyhose mask over my head and turn back
around while leveling a replica of a semiautomatic pistol in

their direction. I then ask them to take a look at my face again. This is the face of a man who, on March 20th, 1992, walked into the First Tier National Bank, pointed a semiautomatic pistol at the face of the teller, and demanded all of the '20s, '50s and hundreds – my first of five armed bank robberies committed over a six-month crime spree. Again, I ask them to please take a close look at my face.

In my life, I have worn both faces. The transformation between the two – suicidal, drug-addicted, bank robber to what I am today – took place gradually over 7 1/2 years within the confines of a federal prison. I use this opening because it grabs my audience by the throat. Surely the clean-cut, suit-sporting, accountant-like man standing before them would be more likely to pull out a flip chart than a deadly weapon, right? After all, my introduction paints a picture of an all-American boy whose academic credentials have placed him on both the Dean's and President's List. But, I do it because I need their attention. I do it because, if I can meet every set of eyes while I am telling my story, and if they listen to my story, not a single person in the room will leave unchanged.

In Roman mythology, there is a god with two faces named Janus. He is the god of gates and the god of beginnings and is depicted with two faces so that he can look forward and look back. I think about him often because my story involves the two faces of my past and my future. It is a story of creating new beginnings and a story of passing through a gate, representative of both the cold, real prison bars that I was behind for a large portion of my life and the threshold I crossed when I left my past and chose my future. As you read this book, I want you to remember Janus.

Who are you now? Who do you want to be? What has kept you from being the person that you want to be? I believe that human beings can adapt to any type of adversity and I believe that we all have room to make some positive change in our lives. This book is for those of you who are standing at the gate of your new beginning, looking at the past and preparing to choose a future as the person that you want to be. It is my hope that you can learn from my story and I can help you to embrace change and take that first step.

Am I proud of the fact that I went to prison? Absolutely not. Do I feel remorse for my victims, and for the pain and shame that was borne by my family? Certainly. But, am I proud of the fact that I took a desperate situation and turned it into the life I lead today? Definitely. Do I believe that my struggles, accomplishments and life lessons can benefit everyday people in everyday lives? Absolutely.

That is why I wrote this book and that is why I spread my message and story to as many people as possible. Over the next 12 chapters as I share my story with you – my ups and downs, good times and bad times – I ask that you read my words not as coming from a bank robber turned speaker, but coming from a man telling you that you can be the person you always dreamed you could be.

Acknowledgements

I am so very grateful to the numerous people who have accompanied and enabled me on the road to becoming a professional speaker, and now an author. My deepest gratitude goes out to:

The late Robert Henry and his family- Marilyn, Patrick and Brent. Robert was my first mentor, believer and door opener in this business. His family welcomed me into their home as if I was one of their own- I will always be grateful to you all, and Robert, I look up at you and smile.

To Carl Hammerschlag and his family. As my second papa, he took over where Robert left off, and has been my confidant, springboard and believer in all that I do. And since marrying one of his "babies", my life has been blessed with a whole new clan that I proudly call family.

To Bill and Marge Johnson. What rough edges Robert and Carl didn't polish, Bill worked into something that was at least presentable. I so very much appreciate his honesty and determination- I also appreciate that Marge was there to keep him in line.

To Wynette Marbut, Robert's secretary and my forever friend. The support and love has been felt for so many years. Thanks for believing.

To Steven Cohen and Aaron Chandler, who through their creative juices and technical support have made me look smarter than I am!

To the National Speakers Association- a group who took a chance on me when all others rejected and discarded my dreams. I would not be where I am today if not for the generosity of its members.

And to all my family and friends who have always supported me.

PART 1:
Choices

Chapter 1: From Cub Scout to Con

"Everything you have in your life is there because you attracted it."
-Mike Wickett

We all made choices to get where we are today. If we stand at the gate of change and look back, some of us can pinpoint an exact moment when things started to go wrong. For others, that moment may be blurred, and all we know is that we have spun out of control since. For me it was a little of both.

How did I come to the point of robbing banks? How did I come to a time in my life where I was willing to point a gun in someone's face and demand his or her money? I can assure you that I did not aspire to become a bank robber growing up. I did not walk into kindergarten career day and say, "When I grow up I want to spend a large chunk of my life in prison and cause my family a great deal of pain." That was, however, the path that I chose.

Believe it or not, I was once an honor role student. I played baseball and football so well that even when I was very young my coaches and parents thought I might go pro one day. I was surrounded by my teammates and friends and coaches encouraging me to do as well as I could. That was my ambition. I wanted to be a professional ball player.

Then, when I was 14 years old, we moved to an entirely different city in an entirely different state and everything changed.

If you've ever moved, you may already be familiar with some of the dynamics of making new friends. For the most part, there is an initiation process. To get in with the cool kids, you have to show them that you're cool. To get in with the jocks, you have to be a good athlete. But, to get in with the "bad kids," all you have to do is be bad. Had I been able to join up with a baseball or football team as soon as I moved I might never have had to make a choice about whom I was going to be. But without that path, my choices were to wait until the school year and sports seasons began or make friends immediately with the kids who were most readily available to me – the "bad kids." I made a choice – the easy one.

Looking back, I can directly link my crimes and incarceration to the decisions I made as a teenager, and in particular, my decision to experiment with drugs. What started out as casual marijuana use, just occasionally on the weekends, soon grew into greater frequency and harder drugs. Before I knew it, and I'm here to tell you it seemed like overnight, drugs became the most important thing in my life. Within the span of two years every event, intention, and action within my existence surrounded acquiring and using drugs. There was not a single aspect of my life that was not affected by drug use.

I eked my way out of high school with C's and D's and immediately turned to the only profession that could feed my habit, and at the same time pay the bills. I dealt drugs. It was obvious that this was the only occupation that would allow me to feed a habit that had now grown to the point of daily use, and to the ingestion of nearly every hard drug available on the streets.

Two years out of high school I met a girl who was foolish enough to marry me, and we had a son. Bringing a child into this world is supposed to be a beautiful thing. At that time, bringing Eric into this world was not. I would look into his crib knowing that I had just helped create a new life, a new person whom I would hurt, whom I would later abandon, a person whom I would add to the long list of those who were devastated by my drug addiction. Bringing my son into this world should have been the most beautiful event in my life. With my addiction tucked firmly at the top of my priority list, I saw that it wasn't. I made a choice. I could have chosen my family...my son...sobriety. I chose drugs. It was easier.

After four years of putting up with my lying, cheating and drug addicted ways, my wife filed for divorce and won primary custody of my son. I didn't think that there was more downhill still available in my life, but I quickly discovered that the gutter has amazing depth.

I chose to leave the small town where my son and ex-wife resided, but found I had nowhere to turn and nowhere to go. My addiction had now reached the point where I literally could not hold any type of job. Not only did a position not exist which could support my daily intake, but I had also reached the point where I stayed so high throughout the day that I could not perform even the simplest of tasks.

For me, robbing banks was a no-brainer. It was a win-win situation. Either I came out of that bank with enough money to feed my addiction for another 30 days or the police showed up, in which case I would force a confrontation and make them take my life. These days they have a catchy term for what I was doing – "suicide by cop." At the time, however, all I knew was that I wanted the police to do something I did not have the courage to do myself.

I'm not going to tell you that my decision to rob banks came without any difficulty. There remained a small part within me that realized that what I was doing was very wrong, that what I was doing was outside of my inner character. There were at least a dozen banks that I entered, gun in waistband, intent on completing the job, only to hand the teller a $10 bill while requesting a roll of quarters. But, confronting my life and going through withdrawals would have been new...unknown...hard. Drugs or death was much easier. I had been taking that path for eight years and knew exactly what to expect.

Then the unexpected happened. Rather than getting myself killed, I was caught, convicted and sentenced to thirteen years in federal prison.

◆◆◆

Some say forget about your past and concentrate on your future, but for those who are looking to make a change, that is tantamount to sticking your head in the sand. As they say, those who forget about history are bound to repeat it.

I think that in order to move forward, we must first recognize where we come from. That means confronting your wrongs and accepting responsibility and it can be painful. That pain makes us fool ourselves. It makes us point fingers, contrive excuses, and it locks us inside a prison where there can be no change.

Have you ever wondered why they make addicts introduce themselves at meetings as addicts? "Hi, my name is Jim and I'm a drug addict." It's because if we say our secrets out loud, it's not a secret. If it's not a secret, we have to deal with it.

Drug addicts are great con artists. It's an important part of the addiction because in addition to fooling our friends and family, we have to fool ourselves. We tell ourselves we're fine, we don't need any help, it's not affecting our work, it's not affecting our families, and we do it because the truth is too terrible.

My first wife brought my family together for an intervention once. I came home to a room full of family, friends, co-workers, and my boss. For every excuse that I gave they had a reply.

"I can't go to rehab now, I have to work."

"That's OK Troy, you can have the time off," replied my boss.

"I have to be here to tend to the livestock."

"That's OK," said my neighbors. "We'll pitch in and help."

"I don't have anything packed."

"I've packed a bag for you," said my wife and, after several more attempts at excuses that they had already thought of, off we went.

They prepare families of drug addicts to cover all of the bases like that, because addicts always have excuses. We have them because it's *easier* to say, "I have to work." It sounds rational and responsible. The alternative, the truth that is screaming through our heads is just too awful. I mean, how could anyone, drug addict included, look their families in the eyes, look at themselves in the mirror and say the truth, "I can't go to rehab until I've had one more hit. I choose drugs over you, me- everyone and everything. I am willing to steal from you, jeopardize your safety, and leave you without your son, husband, father in exchange for my next hit."

Someone recently asked me why, when I was making all of those pivotal decisions in my life, couldn't I take the mask of the bank robber off or stop using drugs. Back then, while I was living in the world of drugs and crime, I had dozens of excuses. Looking back now from my life as a clean, law-abiding citizen, however, I realize that the question shouldn't be "Why couldn't I," but rather "Why didn't I?" It was never a question of can or can't. I'm proof today that I could have all along. The simple answer is that I chose not to. To quit, I would have had to admit I was addicted. To admit I was addicted would mean that I had to look at my actions as an addict. To look at my actions, would have been too horrible for me to bear. To become the man I wanted to be, I had to let my secret out. I had to acknowledge the person I had been and I had to claim the pain that I had caused everyone. This is what I mean by confronting your past and claiming responsibility.

Maybe you're battling an addiction like I was. Maybe the thing you want to change most about yourself is your weight, job or education. Whatever it is, to claim your past, you have to take away all of the reasons that you give yourself and others for being in the situation you are in, claim responsibility for your past, and tell yourself that it is not good enough going forward. If I throw my hands up and say that I was a drug addict and bank robber because I was a victim of a move when I was a teenager and lost my support network, there will always be people there to pat me on the back and say, "Poor Troy," but it will never help me get better because you can't improve yourself by giving your power away. I have to own my decisions. If I claim them, no matter how bad they are I claim the power that I have always had to control my destiny and to make the changes that I want to make in my life.

Try it out. "It was not my mother making me finish all of the food on my plate that makes me overeat; I do it." "Stress does not make me drink; I do." "My boss is not holding me back in my career; I am." "I am not a victim of my past or present who cannot control my future, I choose to take back that power." Say it over and over again, say it to another person, but say it until you can feel the weight of the secret being lifted from your shoulders. Sometimes the hardest part is putting aside the excuses and honestly claiming it for yourself, but it can also be the most freeing.

Chapter 2: Juvenile Injustice

"The person who sees what he wants to see, regardless of what appears, will some day experience in the outer what he has so faithfully seen within."
                                                        -Ernest Holmes

For every change, there is one pivotal point. The point where status quo is abandoned and an entirely new direction chosen. The laws of physics state that objects in motion tend to stay in motion. This applies to life changes as well. To stop or redirect that object takes power and effort just as life changes do. Reversing a trend that you have spent a lifetime building can take a great deal of power, but sometimes great power is wrapped in very small packages.

May 7th, 1993. To that point in my life, it proved to be the hardest day I would ever face. That was the day I stood before a federal judge and was told that I would spend the next 13 years in federal prison. The next 157 months of my life were going to be spent as an incarcerated felon. To that date, it was the hardest day of my life...but it was nothing compared to the next.

May 8th, 1993. That was the day that I had to call my, then seven-year-old, son Eric and let him know that his dad was not going to be available to him for a very long time. "Incarceration" is a hard enough concept for an adult to fathom. For a seven-year-old child, a third grader, it's impossible. Eric could not comprehend the span of 13 years. How do you understand an amount of time that is twice that of your age? All he wanted to know was whether he was going to be able to come spend next summer vacation with me, as had been the case the prior three years.

"No Eric, you won't be coming to spend next summer vacation with me."

"Well how about the one after that Dad?"

"No Eric, not that one either."

"Well for sure the one after that, right Dad?"

"No Eric, not the one after that either."

After asking a few more times, he finally asked, "When do I get to come spend the summer with you, Dad?"

"Maybe the one when you turn eighteen Eric. That will be the next time you get to spend a summer vacation with your Daddy."

My son lived in a very small midwestern town. EVERYBODY knew his business. EVERYBODY knew where his daddy was. EVERBODY knew his dad was a convict. Kids can be extremely cruel, and I knew that what I had done would cause my son to be teased, tormented and ridiculed for years to come. I had let him down throughout his life and going to prison was going to make it even worse.

I dreaded the question that I knew would always hang in his eyes, the "Why?" that I would never be able to answer, but the first time I saw Eric in the prison visiting room I came around the corner to hear my son asking a guard a very different question. "If you won't let my dad spend the night with me at the hotel tonight, can I spend the night in here with him?"

It hit me like a ton of bricks. Despite everything my son had just gone through he still wanted to stay the night here with me in prison. Despite all of the slamming steel doors behind him, despite having to take off his belt and shoes while going through a metal detector, and despite, at seven years old, being "patted down" to see that he wasn't smuggling in contraband, I was still a hero in his eyes. I was still his Daddy no matter where I was and what I did. On that day when he visited, I went from being a nameless, faceless, convict among 1,200 inmates – Evans #24291-013 – to being a hero. I wanted to grab him, squeeze him and say thank you for still loving me!

That day I came to two very important realizations. Number one, drugs had become more important to me than the most important person in my life. It really had become that simple – drugs meant more to me than my son did. And, number two, I was breaking a long-standing tradition. The tradition of my great grandfather being there for my grandfather, my grandfather being there for my Dad and my Dad being there for me. Instead of being there for my son, I gave him ridicule at school, an absent father and the eternal question that was always on the tip of his tongue no matter how cheerful he tried to be – "Why did you leave me?"

Incarceration, detention, and prison – they all mean the same thing. They are deprivation. My son had been deprived of his father for all seven years of his life. I was looking with fear at a thirteen year prison sentence having never realized that my son had been born into a prison of his own, his only crime being that he was born to a father who had made drugs his priority. And yet, I heard him asking again and again if he could be with me. I heard the hope in his voice for a father who had never even been very good at it and I decided right then and there that I was going to be a better man. Steel bars or no, I was going to be as close to the father that my son deserved as I could possibly be. If my son still had hope for me, then I could have hope as well.

That was it. That was my pivotal point.

Like I said before, sometimes the power that you need comes in small packages. For me, it was the hope of a child. Great things can be learned from children.

Remember when you were a child? Did you believe that you could be anything you wanted when you grew up? When did you stop believing that?

I saw hope for my future reflected in my son's image of me. Once I caught a glimmer of that hope, I began to see it when

I looked at the reflection in the mirror. He taught me that. He taught me to start believing that anything was possible again. He taught me to live my life with the hope of a child.

How many times have you wanted to do something, to make a change in your life only to get bogged down with all of the reasons why it could never happen. You may say, "I want to go back and get my degree." Then you start to hear the little voice in the back of your head. "How can I go to class around my work schedule?" "Who will watch the kids?" "I'm too old to go back to school." And suddenly you realize you have been defeated before you've even picked up a course catalog. I have news for you. It wasn't the job, the kids or the missed opportunity that defeated you. It was the little voice – the excuses that let you avoid the situation rather than dealing with it. They are the same excuses that cover up the real question – "What if I can't?"

I had listened to that little voice all of my life telling me why I couldn't give up drugs, get a job, and love my family. "What if I failed?" "No one would hire me anyway." "My family was better off without me." The little voice was always with me. But, the day that I saw hope reflected in my child's face, that little voice started getting fainter and fainter and the possibility of earning the hero status that my son had already bestowed upon me became greater and greater. For the first time in my life, I was truly focused on what was most important and it was all due to a child's hope, not my son's, but the hope that had been reawakened in me.

Think, for a moment, about what it was like to have the hope and confidence of a child who knew that anything was possible. Now, do yourself a favor. Go over to a mirror and tell yourself whom you could be. "I could be a non-smoker." "I could be the best salesman in my company." "I could be a college graduate." "I could be the parent that my child deserves." If you hear that little voice start to creep in, say it to yourself again. In fact every time you hear that voice, find yourself a mirror and say it again. Drown that little voice out and create your own pivotal point. The point where the little voice no longer calls the shots. You do.

If you can do just that, you have stepped through that gate onto the path to becoming the person that you always wanted to be.

Chapter 3: Awakened Within the Walls

"When one door closes, another opens; but we often look so long and so regretfully at the closed door that we do not see the one which has opened for us."

-Alexander Graham Bell

Hope is a powerful thing. It has near euphoric qualities, but hope alone cannot get you to your goal. That is what I found out during the next few days. The days that I knew I was going to prison but had no idea what to expect.

I had spent the last eight months waiting for sentencing in a federal detention facility while going through the trial process. "Federal Detention Facility" sounds a lot like prison, but there are a few integral differences.

Within the walls of a federal prison, drugs are more easily obtained than they are on the streets. Heroin overdose is a regular occurrence, bloodshed over drug deals gone bad take place routinely, and stemming the drug flow into the institution is a constant battle for the staff. I wasn't ready to face that availability on my own. That eight-month period within the detention facility gave me a chance to clear my head, to think rationally, and to make a conscious decision to turn my life around without the ready availability of drugs that the prison system would have to offer. That was the best and only leg up that the system gave me.

Without the drugs, I gained clarity. With that clarity, came some of the scariest moments of my life. I had no idea what to expect when I arrived at my permanent facility. Faced with a 13-year prison sentence, I'm sure you can imagine the apprehension and fear that I felt. This was pure, unadulterated reality, no drug haze to stifle the fear. My brain cells were operating to full capacity and, for the first time in years, I knew true fear. My son had given my life value again. In the short period of time I had within the relative safety of the detention facility I went from being a suicidal drug addict to a man with too much to lose and I was facing the legends of prison.

I, like everyone else, had heard stories of the terrors that take place inside prison walls, the beatings, the rapes, and the murders. The funny thing was that it wasn't any one of those things that kept me awake at night. It was all of them and none of them and various combinations. What would it be like? Would it be as Hollywood portrayed it in the movies? Would I be beaten, stabbed, forced into a gang? All I knew was that I wasn't looking forward to fresh meat orientation and whatever that might have implied. Then it dawned on me. My greatest fear was not simply that I would have to face all of these potential threats, but that if I were to carry through with my promise to my son, and myself I would have to do it without the drugs.

During that time, I thought about drugs a lot. I craved the numbness. I wanted that familiar switch that I could flick and make all of my worries go away. But somewhere a certain knowledge came with my newfound clarity that told me that this was a challenge that I needed to face head on if I was ever going to be able to come out of it the man that I wanted to be. So, on the day that I first entered the Florence Federal Correctional Institution, that was the way that I approached it. Head up, with a brave face. Was I scared? You can't begin to imagine. But since then, I have learned that the only way to face change is to embrace it, welcome it, and learn to love it with your head up and a brave face.

◆◆◆

One of the most amazing things that I witnessed throughout my incarceration is what I call "dead time." It seemed to physically hang in the air, as though it were something you could touch or feel around you. When I first arrived in prison I would sit in the common areas and watch guys play cards, play dominos, and watch TV. Some of them would spend their entire sentences doing the same thing, for up to 16 hours a day, day after day, week after week, month after month, year after year. Some of them doing this in five, ten, fifteen, even twenty year stretches. I watched them and made a decision that this was not the way I was going to spend the next eleven and one half years of my life. This was not going to keep me on my path and it certainly wasn't going to help me pay the bills once I was out. That's when I realized that being inside walls and razor wire was not the prison, dead time was.

While inside, I knew that dead time was not good enough for me. The irony is that I had been serving my dead time before I ever got to prison. I just never recognized it. Now that I do,

I notice that free people choose to do it every day. They choose it without ever knowing that they are doing it. We sit on our couches, trudge into jobs we don't like, live as people that we don't want to be and we do it day after day, week after week, month after month, year after year. We construct our own prisons and they are not made out of bricks and mortar or razor wire but of fear of change and the excuses it breeds – the little voice.

It's funny, I have to be one of a very few people in this world who can make a statement such as this: The very worst thing that ever happened to me in my life, going to prison, is at the same time the very best thing that ever happened to me. There is no doubt in my mind that if I had not been caught, convicted and incarcerated, I would be dead. There's also no doubt in my mind that if I had not been forced to confront great changes and the overwhelming fear that was associated with them, I could never have become the man I am today. I would never have been awakened from my dead time.

The fear of the unknown keeps us from reaching out, from taking chances, from exploring new possibilities, from pushing ourselves to realize our full potential. After all, we might not succeed. We might lose our comfort zone. We might CHANGE! ...Or, we could succeed. We might benefit. And, we might be one step closer to being the people we want to be.

I had help thanks to the officers who arrested me without allowing me to forfeit my life. Only by being forced into this harsh environment was I finally going to make some changes, finally going to face my past. Once I did that, I learned that facing change head on and learning to love it made it possible for me to do anything I set my mind to. It is not enough to have hope, that is just the first step. It is the courage to face and embrace change that helps you make the second step and then what you have is something very powerful – momentum.

Chapter 4: Never Easy

"If you want something you have never had, you have to do something you have never done."

-Mike Murdock

My son had helped me take my first step and I had found new courage to face my fears and begin building momentum, but then something happened that almost stopped me dead in my tracks, literally.

Since I happened to be arrested in Denver, Colorado, I was put on trial 90 miles from the brand new Federal Correctional Complex in Florence, Colorado. The same complex that at one time held Timothy McVeigh and Terry Nichols. Because this new facility was opening up and because they needed bodies, this is where I was sent. And, because I was sent to FCI Florence, I was lucky enough to be situated thirty miles away from home – Colorado Springs. I was just thirty miles from my family, thirty miles from my friends, and thirty miles from the most important people in my life.

Despite all of my problems, my parents had always been supportive of me in the ways that they could. They had intervened and paid for rehabilitation stays several times, forgiven me for stealing from them on countless occasions, and continued to love me even as I wore away at any faith they could have that I would ever do right. But, most

23

importantly, they made the thirty-mile drive and continued to support me while I was going through the roughest years of my life in prison.

This close proximity allowed me frequent visits, almost every weekend. This wasn't the norm. Ninety percent of the inmates that I was incarcerated with were from different parts of the country – California, New York, Chicago, Texas, spread throughout the United States. My family's proximity was a blessing to me, but it almost turned into a curse.

Within the Federal prison system, gangs run the institutions. As the gangs go, so goes the prison. The Aryan Brotherhood, the Mexican Mafia, the Bloods, the Crips – they dictate what happens behind the walls of many Federal prisons. When some of these gang members discovered the frequency of my visits I was approached and was told that I was going to smuggle drugs into the institution, through the visiting room, using my family and my friends as mules or they were going to kill me.

Each was carrying a shank which is basically a weapon made out of everyday objects found in a prison or, as I like to refer to them, the best and brightest products of prison ingenuity. The first guy is carrying a toothbrush. Yes indeed, I said a toothbrush. The difference between this toothbrush and the everyday toothbrush we all use each morning is that this toothbrush has one end filed to a very sharp point and the other wrapped in duct tape to resemble a handle. The second one is carrying a pork chop bone. Once again, yes you read correctly, a pork chop bone. They take the long end of the bone and again they grind it down on the concrete to a very fine point and use the large portion of the bone as a handle that fits nicely in the palm of the hand. This tool is most effective from behind when stuck in the artery of the neck. The third guy is carrying a 16- penny nail driven through a six-inch piece of a broom handle. These are the tools by which they take each other's lives in prison. They were serious. They didn't care that this could mean more time for me, or incarceration for my family and/or friends if we were caught. I was given a choice…if you could call it that.

As they enter my cell, I'm terrified. My first reaction was that I would do anything they say, I wanted to live. But when they gave me their ultimatum something much stronger than fear came over me. I saw the face of my son and remembered how he was committed to me regardless of where I was. I thought about my Mom and my Dad, and the commitment I made to them to turn my life around, and how it had always been my family that was sacrificed in the past. I thought about how I wanted to be that person that my son saw me to be and that my parents were hoping I'd be. And, I remembered something that my dad always used to say. A saying which I lost track of during my teens and early 20's, but came back to me in that moment. What my dad used to say was this, "Anything in this life which is really worthwhile, which is REALLY worthwhile, is never easy."

All my life I had always taken the easy road. The easy road is the road of drug use. The easy road is a road of lying, cheating and stealing. Anybody can do these things, it takes no type of special person to do them; anyone can take this easy road. The more difficult road is a road of self-respect, a road of believing in you. It's a road of often standing to one side and feeling alone when it seems that everyone else is heading in a different direction or passing you by, but knowing in your head and in your heart that what you are doing is the right thing.

Peer pressure was the number one driving force in my becoming involved with drugs and in heading down the wrong path as a teenager. Everyone wants to be liked, everyone wants to be accepted. It was easier to go along with the pressure rather than stand alone against it. In prison that pressure is magnified one hundred fold. In prison, not fitting in could cost you your life.

For fourteen years I had taken the easy road. This was my time to make a stand. I would choose my family over myself. I would choose my integrity before asking my family to bail me out again. I would choose to be true to the goal of becoming the person I wanted to be. I would choose death before I would ever utter that request.

What happened next? I was saved. The jingle of keys came to us from down the corridor; a guard was on the way. When the gang members heard that jingle, that sweet, wonderful jingle, they took their shanks and tossed them under my mattress. You're only allowed to have two inmates in a cell at any one time so the guard sticks his head in and says, "Evans, what are these guys doing in your cell?" I tell the guard, "They're not doing anything, we're just kickin' it, they're not doing anything at all."

He ordered them out of the cell, and five minutes later I gathered up their shanks and one at a time took them back to their owners, explaining that they had forgotten something. They never bothered me again. Whether it was because I didn't tell the guard what they were doing in my cell that afternoon, or whether it was the fact that they could see in my eyes that I was no longer going to take that easy road and they were going to have to do the job they set out to do, they never bothered me again.

I felt like I was rewarded for that decision. I felt as though it was the decision itself that had saved me. I had proven to myself that I was finally ready to put others ahead of myself. But above that, I had chosen myself, as I wanted to be, over the self that I had been. That was no longer good enough for me. I was ready to claim my integrity, cease making excuses, and quit taking advantage of my family's love for the sake of my own survival.

◆◆◆

The decision between taking the easy road and staying true to myself was a choice that I had to make daily and continue to make day by day. I suspect that this is the case in many of our lives. The choice is not always as drastic as life and death, but is as simple as choosing an excuse over what you know is right for you. Everyday events can be interwoven with conscious or unconscious decisions and actions that lead us down the easier path. Many people suffer from addictions, abusive relationships, overeating, lack of exercise, overworking. The list goes on and on. These "prisons within ourselves" are just as confining as the steel bars and razor wire that kept me locked up.

Find your hope, embrace change, but know that you will have to follow it up with determination. Determination to be true to yourself as you want to be. Determination to hold that value of yourself high enough to make any price worth it. If you can find that determination, you will win by having just made the decision. You'll gain the pride that makes the first pound you lose sweeter than the cookies you gave up for it; the self worth that makes the first day you spend without fear of being beaten feel safer than having the possessions you left behind; the integrity that makes the first day of sobriety with your family more intoxicating than an evening of drinking alone. Free yourselves from these prisons by taking the more difficult road, that road of self-respect, the road to a brighter future, the road to the life you want to live.

Chapter 5: Power and Responsibility in Prison

"The golden opportunity you are seeking is in yourself. It is not in your environment; it is not in luck or chance, or the help of others; it is in yourself alone."

-Orison Swett Marden

As I mentioned earlier, my son drove the first phase of my "awakening." When I discovered that I had this power to influence Eric in a positive direction it gave me a renewed sense of hope, a sense of purpose, a belief that the next several years would be something other than just wasted time, a sense that some good could come out of my being imprisoned. For me it would be education. Education was going to be my saving grace.

My child's hope was telling me that I was still the person who had, at one time in life, had a straight A report card. I remembered how proud I had been to bring home those report cards and how proud my parents had been of me. I remembered a teacher taking me aside when I first started to go downhill and telling me that I was too good for that. And, I looked forward and knew that when I got out of prison, an ex-con and an ex-drug addict, I was going to need all the help that I could get to function in society again. Education would be the means by which I could turn a very negative situation into a life change for the positive. The bonus was that education was something my son and I could do together. I was excited and ready to get started right away, but I soon learned that I had challenges to face before I could even open my first book.

While some correctional institutions offer work programs, limited vocational programs, and very limited educational opportunities, the bottom line remains that today's institutions are based more on incarceration than they are on rehabilitation. Federal Pell grants are no longer available to either federal or state inmates, and what meager budgets most institutions are forced to work with are already overburdened with security issues, leaving little or nothing for education or rehabilitation.

I have read studies stating that the re-arrest rate of individuals who come out of prison with just two years of college is at 10 percent. This compares to a rate of over 60 percent for those who walk out of the prison gates with no education whatsoever. Conservative estimates put costs to incarcerate an individual for a year at $35,000. It would cost a small fraction of that to educate that same individual, and in the long run would prove to be both a savings monetarily, and a potentially enormous benefit to society. I could make an argument that we are not doing society a favor in locking up criminals time and again without offering them any rehabilitation, education or means to rebuild and better themselves. But, I can tell you as fact, there was no way I was going to become the man I wanted to be if the only post-incarceration job skills available to me were going to be learned from the convicts I was doing time with.

Education was tantamount to the life I wanted to lead. I had made my decision and I had momentum and determination, but no funding, so I turned to plan B. If Congress wasn't going to give me a chance to improve myself while I was in prison, I would create that window of opportunity for myself. I started committing every second of my free time to my goal. Every day for six months, every free minute I had, fourteen to sixteen hours a day, day after day, I sat at my tiny little prison desk in my tiny little prison cell, filling out applications, writing essays, begging, pleading, and selling myself to every private scholarship around the country that I even remotely qualified for. I knew that I was a con. I was a felon. No one was waiting in line to take a chance on me. I knew that I would have to convince them and I knew that it was going to be hard, very hard. I got used to reading the words, "sorry"..."not qualified"..."no." Each day at mail call I received a stack of rejection letters...until July 16th, 1997.

At that point, I had been incarcerated for four and one half years. I spent those years in a cage and had grown accustomed, as well as one can, to my environment, to the daily disappointments, and to the daily pep talks that would put me back at my desk filling out applications. There was nothing special about this particular day, just going about my everyday prison routine, when a guard sticks his head in my cell. He informs me that my counselor wants to see me immediately. I shuffle down the hallway to my counselor's office and am told, "Evans sit down, I got a phone call on you today from a guy in Auburn, Alabama. He's a scholarship committee chairman, and his association is interested in helping you with your schooling."

I couldn't believe it. I went over the words in my head again. Yes, he had just told me that I had earned a scholarship. The size didn't matter. In spite of all of the wrong paths I had chosen in the past, I had convinced someone, in fact a whole committee of someone's, to believe in me.

A week later I received a letter from Robert Henry, the scholarship committee chairman, and a check for one class. The letter informed me that although I did not meet one single criteria specified in qualifying for the scholarship, the committee was so impressed with what I was trying to accomplish that they were going to award me a special stipend. I took that one class and I sent the association my report card. They then sent me a check for two more classes and it snowballed from there.

When I landed that first scholarship, Eric took a keen interest in the fact that his dad was going to school. He asked that I send him my graded papers. I think he wanted to see for himself that his dad was actually going to school like he was. After that Eric showed a renewed interest in his own schooling, and we began to mail our graded papers, test scores, and report cards back and forth. He would send me his papers with the little stars, the smiley faces and the teacher comments. I would send him my test scores, report cards and term papers along with the professor comments. It became a competition with us, something that we could do together, something that we could share. As we talked on the phone weekly we would rib each other when one wouldn't do so well on a test or assignment. My education became a way for me to stay connected with my son, to share something with him, to be a part of his life. I wasn't tossing a baseball back and forth with my boy, but I was doing something with him. You know what I'm saying? I was doing something with my son.

My continuing education and the fact that I was attempting to turn my life around, combined with the positive strides I was making toward becoming a new person, had an effect on others as well. Those on the outside that were following my progress, many of them family and friends who had given up on me long before, suddenly began to ask how I was doing. I was able to start laying a foundation of trust with them again.

My fellow inmates began to notice what I was doing and took an interest. Before I knew it, I had become a prison role model. In fact, the same three inmates who had threatened me with shanks previously visited me, but this time, instead of carrying weapons, they came with a request to help them do the same thing I was doing. Those three gang members who rolled in on me, the gang members who came there to take my life if I wasn't willing to sling their drugs, now looked to me to save them.

I had turned my life around one hundred and eighty degrees. I went from a worthless drug addict to a father to my child, a son to my parents, a model of success to a scholarship program, and a role model to my fellow inmates who were starting to choose education over dead time.

I had given myself the best present that I could have received. I used hope to reclaim my self-worth. Then I put my self-worth out to the world until I convinced a scholarship committee to see potential. From potential, I built a full scholarship program and a relationship with my son. From my accomplishments I taught my parents and loved ones to listen to the hope in their hearts rather than the pessimism of experience. And from there, my worth branched out to people who would never have known who I was, including you reading this book, if I had not believed in myself first.

◆◆◆

Did you know that Americans have spent billions of dollars on the diet and addiction industries, many of them without any success? The reason for that is that the industries target people who have trouble taking that first step of believing in themselves. In fact, many of the buyers are people who have fallen into a spiral of despair and self-loathing and are using an impulse purchase of a product to pull them back out. In the time it takes to read a credit card number over the phone, they can instantly feel better about having taken a first step. The problem is that it is the wrong first step. The one and only first step that will make you successful is believing in yourself.

Try it. You'll be amazed at how quickly self-worth and self-confidence spread. Take that mantra that you told yourself in the mirror earlier, change it from "I could be" to "I am" and put it out to the world. Start believing it yourself and acting on it. Commit to it with determination and show people by your actions that you can be the person that you want to be. If the path is difficult, want it more. As my father would say, nothing in life that is really worth having is ever easy. Use the hope, confront your fear of change, be determined, claim your worth out loud and put one foot in front of the other until you reach your goal. If you are scared, give yourself a small goal at first. Remember, my first success was only enough money for one class. The end result was two college degrees. I guarantee that once you've tasted a little success, you'll learn to crave it and it will come to you more naturally.

PART 2:
Some Words of Warning

"Many of life's failures are men who did not realize how close they were to success when they gave up."
-Thomas Edison

Chapter 6: Public Image of an Inmate

"A man is not finished when he is defeated;
he's finished when he quits."
-Richard Milhous Nixon

So I'm cruising along now, things are good. I'm making my mom and dad proud. I'm making my brother and sister proud. I'm making my son proud. And I am making my scholarship committee VERY happy. I am two classes away from completing my second degree and am already making plans to start on my Masters when a new warden comes to FCI Florence. He immediately takes a dislike to me. He doesn't like the fact that I am allowed extra computer time, he doesn't like the fact that I'm being allowed extra library time, and he in particular does not like the fact that I'm being allowed to receive videotapes via the mail so that I can take my courses by correspondence. He tells me that this is all coming to an end immediately.

I understand that this warden doesn't know me and has no way of knowing how hard I've worked to accomplish as much as I have, so I turn to the association that has funded my schooling this entire time to plead my case for me. I figure that they have better ground to stand on, not being convicted felons themselves, and they happen to be very well connected in the political arena.

Over the next several weeks over two-dozen senators and congressmen call and write this warden demanding to know why I am not being allowed to complete my second degree. He doesn't like this. He has just had his authority challenged in his own prison by a convicted felon. He is not used to answering to anyone and his back is up against the wall. So he trumps up charges on me, puts me under investigation and throws me in the hole as a risk to the institution's security. All it took was his signature on a couple of forms. All he had to do was make one false accusation and suddenly I was facing up to 90 days in the hole without any justification. To the hole I go.

I've dedicated my life, and this book, to inspiring people to ask more of themselves and more of the world. I have asked you to claim your past, hope as a child, embrace change, steel your determination and believe in yourself. These are the steps along the path to becoming the person you want to be. I would be doing you a great disservice, however, if I did not take a few of chapters to warn you about the obstacles that you may still have ahead. Unfortunately, they often pop up when you least expect them.

By the time the new warden had come to FCI Florence, I thought I had been through the toughest part of the challenge. I was cruising. I had become a different person altogether. I was clean. I was a positive role model for my son and fellow inmates. I had regained my self worth and dignity. I was doing something special.

I think that might be where I was going wrong in the warden's eye.

I'm sure that there was a fear of the special privileges. If I had special privileges, everyone would want them. Of course, this begs the question, why not give them? I've already touched on the statistics of the educated ex-con. What if, at this point, the warden had taken advantage of my work to hold me up as a model to the other prisoners? What if he used me to encourage the other prisoners to better themselves? Might he have been considered a leader? A role model to wardens across the country for having the foresight to see that education can help rehabilitate criminals? We'll never know. He took the easy path and flexed his muscles rather than using his brain.

In Australia they have this saying. If the guy down the street starts acting above his station or gets too big for his britches, they'll say, "ole so and so is being a tall poppy." Basically what they mean is that if someone sticks their head up above the crowd, they are just begging to get cut down. I think that is what the warden thought of me. In his eyes, I was the same addict and bank robber that my file told him I was and he wanted to remind me of it. Bank robbers don't get extra computer time or special privileges, they get hard time. Drug addicts don't get video courses and college degrees, they get all of the punishment that the system can dish out. And, prosecuted felons do not, I repeat, do not question wardens about how they will run their prison either directly or through a bunch of fancy suits on the outside. I was a tall poppy and he was going to mow me down.

People will try to sabotage you. Do not let them. It generally has nothing to do with what you are actually trying to accomplish with your own life, but rather, what it represents to the person who is trying to take your power away. For the warden it was a way to assert his authority in the prison. For others, sabotaging your successes can be a way to make them feel better about their own failures.

A friend once told me about an Oprah Winfrey show that she saw shortly after Oprah had lost all of her weight. Here Oprah had finally accomplished this goal that she had set for herself and what did she get in return? Bags of mail from people who said that they wouldn't watch her show any more. She had changed. She was no longer like them. These people did not hold her up as a role model, a winner of a tough battle. They lashed out in bitterness in an attempt to make their own failures her fault. She had risen above her place and they were going to try to make her feel like less of a person. It was because she had a personal chef. It was because she had a personal trainer. It was because she had money. She was not better than them. She had not earned her success. She was just rich.

I'm not sure what they thought they were doing. I can just see Oprah running down the street to her local bakery, "I must be fat so my fans can feel better about themselves" ...not. What were they trying to accomplish?

Unfortunately, strangers do not always deal this sort of punishment out. From a friend or relative, someone you trust, someone who is supposed to treat you with love, being denounced as a "tall poppy" simply for reaching for a dream can be absolutely devastating. If, rather than lashing out, they use your relationship as a close friend or relative to try to sabotage you, it can be downright heart breaking.

I have been in drug rehabilitation three times in my life. All three were before I went to prison and all three times I failed to be rehabilitated. A couple of times I bought into the program and thought, "This is it, I'm really going to do it this time." Each time, I would walk out of rehab clear-headed, a new man. And, each time, all of my wonderful drug addicted friends would throw me a great big congratulatory party filled with enough drugs to kill me dozens of times over. My friends. My "friends."

So right about now, you may be saying, "Troy, what are you doing? I was so excited, I was so motivated, and you're telling me that the world is against me."

My reply is that, if I didn't tell you these things, I'd be selling you a bill of goods. I've told you about the steps that you can take to become the person you want to be. Let's just consider this chapter a sturdy pair of walking boots to protect against sprained ankles.

Hopefully, you have surrounded yourself with people who want the best for you. If so, you've just gained some added strength in your fight. If not, here's a chance to do some weeding of your own. There are people who are going to see your head rising above the others in the poppy field and not like it. If they are your "friends," be prepared to leave them behind. They are not your friends.

If they are strangers who, for whatever reason, have decided to try to derail you from your dreams, don't let them; that is not their right.

Steel yourself, stick to your path and march forward with determination. This is the point where some people will want to give up and lay down lest they be cut down. Me? I'm taking one of my books with me to the hole.

Chapter 7: From Hole to Whole

"What lies behind us, and what lies before us are tiny matters, compared to what lies within us."
-Ralph Waldo Emerson

The "Hole" is a 6 by 9 foot cell, containing a steel bunk bed, a stainless-steel toilet connected to a stainless-steel sink, and a stainless-steel shower. You're locked in this cell for 24 hours a day, with the exception of one hour a day when you are sometimes, and I want to reiterate, sometimes, let out to pace back and forth in what looks like a small dog kennel.

The people I'm in the hole with are the troublemakers of the institution; many of them are mentally challenged and probably shouldn't be within the confines of a traditional prison setting. Hour after hour, day after day, week after week they beat on the doors and scream. There is never a quiet moment. You never get any proper rest, but instead learn to catch a few winks as it subsides to a dull roar. The steel door which provides the entrance into the cells contains a small slit in the center, and when opened up provides the means through which they slide your food tray into the cell. As I stated previously, many of those that I'm in the hole with are looking for trouble. You may be minding your own business and the next thing you know, your psychopath roommate decides that it is a good idea to throw a cup full of urine and feces in the guards' faces when they open up the slot to slide in the food tray. What do the guards do? They do what most of us would do if that were done to us. They "suit up" and come in with their batons. You don't have any control over who your cellmate is when you're in the hole, and you better hope it wasn't your cellmate who decided to pull this because you're taking a beating right along with him. The guards don't know whose arm it was that came out of that slot and frankly they really don't care. And don't think the guards forget about these incidents anytime soon. For the next two weeks, at least, that slot isn't staying open for very long. Your food tray is coming in on the fly. I don't know how you feel about eating food off a concrete floor shared by the human waste tosser, but believe me, when you're hungry enough you'll eat food off of anything.

Two months I'm in this setting. Sixty days I'm living in this tiny cage along with the animals of FCI Florence. I'm losing weight, I've become pale, and I've read the same book six times. Up to that point I had always believed that things happened for a reason, but I have to tell you my faith is being tested here. I had always believed that I could learn something from any situation I was placed in, but at this point, the little voice is starting to come through again, "Why is this happening to you Troy? All you're trying to do is improve yourself, all you're trying to do is give yourself a chance to succeed when you're released, all you're trying to do is get an education. Why is this happening? Why do you even bother?"

They, this ubiquitous they, continue to tell me I'm under investigation but they won't tell me for what. I'm faced with the possibility of at least another 30 days before anyone even has to review my situation. And then it happens. The only thing that can make the situation any worse. They inform me that I'm being shipped to FCI Englewood, the oldest, nastiest prison within the Federal Bureau of Prisons. Built in 1939 it's like something out of a medieval movie. I'm being shipped to the armpit of all prisons.

Shifted like cattle from one pen to another, I was informed that asbestos removal was making things tighter than usual. Within the individual housing units 150 inmates shared a pod consisting of a common area and individual cubes. The common area is approximately 20 by 40 feet and houses four showers, three sinks, three toilets and a microwave oven. No stalls, no privacy, barely room to breath. On the east wall guys are taking a shower, on the north wall guys are using the bathroom, on the west wall three people are brushing their teeth, and on the south my fellow inmates are lined up to heat their food in the microwave oven. Take a moment to picture this. No stalls, one large open area and all of these different activities taking place right next to one another. Just over five square feet per prisoner, minus the space taken up by the five star amenities. You could feel the room breath.

Of course there was some respite if you could call it that. I was also assigned to a cube. Within this small cube (which I would estimate to be 10 by 12 feet) there were three bunk beds to accommodate my five lovely cellmates and me. My experience at FCI Florence had taught me that it was hard enough to find one guy you can let your guard down around. I couldn't even imagine what this was going to be like.

I'm in this setting for only a very short time before the realization sets in that there's no way I can spend the next five years under these conditions. Again comes the voice "Why is this happening, Troy? Why have you been singled out? Why have you been placed in such a grotesque atmosphere? How are you going to do this time?" I try and keep my outlook as positive as possible. The only way I know to do that is to start over again. I need to feel myself working towards my goals, otherwise, I will start to feel the reality of my new conditions, just barely above that of the hole. I concentrate on staying positive and on the tasks at hand to get me back on track. All the while I am trying to control the voice.

Of course there is plenty to do because, in many ways, I had to start from scratch. First, I had to get permission from Englewood's educational coordinator. I had been in the middle of my last two courses when I was thrown in the hole, so I filled out the paperwork to get my books and coursework sent to me. I also had to write to the school to get permission to resume the classes and convince them to make a special exception for me so that I could complete the class without the video that I was required to watch. After about a month, I received the permissions that I needed, but was informed that all of my coursework and books had been "lost" in the transfer. Of course, I've always suspected that they were probably "lost" the first day that I was thrown in the hole, but regardless of what happened to them, I was responsible for that work and I needed the books to do it. So, I had to repurchase the books, which anyone who has ever had to purchase a textbook knows, is not cheap and I had to rewrite all of the papers that I had completed during the first half of the course.

My work area was a desk in the corner similar to the one in the previous facility. At FCI Florence, however, I had only had one roommate to share a desk with and we worked opposite shifts at the prison furniture plant. At FCI Englewood, I shared with five people who were constantly coming or going. Whether they were writing letters home or doing some other activity that required the use of the desk, I soon found that sometimes sitting on the floor with my books and papers piled around me had to be good enough.

It took me three months to finish my classes and get my second degree. The little voice is starting to get fainter again and I'm starting to contemplate my Masters degree again when I hear my name called over the intercom, "Evans #24291-013 report to the records office immediately." The lady at the records office tells me to shut the door and sit down. I would later discover that FCI Englewood is the only institution within the Federal Bureau of Prisons that has the policy that saved me, the only institution in the entire nation that automatically reviews the sentence computation of every inmate that is transferred into their facility via another facility. She tells me she just got off the phone with the regional office and in reviewing my sentence computation she has found that there's been a mistake. I should not have been sentenced to thirteen years. I should have only been sentenced to eight. I'm going home in ten days.

◆◆◆

I just summarized that whole experience in nine paragraphs. Possibly the most important six months of my life, and they are all right there in nine short paragraphs. The most crucial, desperate moment in my transformation, and we just blew right by it. But there was a warning there. You will be tested; and you will have to choose to pass.

In the first part of this book, I talked about finding your hope and building momentum, but when I was transferred to FCI Englewood, my hopes were challenged, my momentum was taken, and my path was nowhere in sight. For the first time in years, I was hearing that little voice again. My power, my hopes, and my future were being taken from me. I was facing another five years in one of the worst prisons in the U.S. For the first time in years, I started to notice who was dealing drugs inside and how I could get them.

Those situations, the really tough ones that seem to take away all hope and often come up on you in a blink of an eye, are tests, and tests are meant to be hard. I had to choose to pass that test. I had to look desperate times in the face and say, "I am not the person I once was and no matter how difficult life becomes, I will no longer choose that easy path because nothing in life that is worthwhile is ever easy." If I had let my power be taken, if I had gone back to serving dead time, if I had turned back to drugs, the Troy Evans released from FCI Englewood three months later would have been a different person altogether. In those three months, I could have thrown it all away.

You too will be tested. There will be times when you will lose your path. There will be times when you make a choice and find yourself on the wrong path, and there will be times, when you lose your path due to circumstances out of your control. When that happens, you will be tempted to lose hope. You may find yourself slipping into a spiral of self-loathing or cynicism. This is a test, and like any good test, it will be hard.

I cannot give you a map to move forward when you lose your path, but a map does exist. It is the one that you will draw as you travel your path. It may not be able to tell you how to move forward, but it can tell you where you've been. My advice is, if and when you do lose your way, there is never any shame in starting over. In fact, that is often the best way to get back on the path. Go back to the point that you last knew you were on the right path and start again. I had to start the permission process all over again at FCI Englewood. I even had to redo several of my assignments. But, while I was retracing my steps to get back on the right path, I was choosing to pass my test. The same will be true for you. There is no such thing as absolute failure unless you choose it by giving up. Choose to succeed.

Chapter 8: Passing Through Open Gates

"Any fact facing us is not as important as our attitude toward it, for that determines our success or failure."
-Dr. Norman Vincent Peale

The moment of my release, I was filled with overwhelming happiness. I had learned valuable lessons and I had succeeded. I was drug free and educated, I had my family back, and I had my whole life ahead of me. But, I soon found out that freedom itself was a challenge.

The first night of my release, my sister picked me up at the gates a free man for the first time in many, many years. It was an extremely strange feeling to come and go as I wanted. There were trees around me, a dog ran by, I heard a kid laugh, and I had an ice cream cone. To celebrate, my sister took me to downtown Denver for dinner and introduced me to sushi. I had never heard of such a thing and the thought seemed repugnant, but compared to what I had been fed for the last several years I knew there was no way it could kill me. She dropped me off in the middle of downtown Denver as she went to park the car. There I stood, lights flashing, cars passing, crowds of people walking by me. The stimulation was overwhelming. I was frozen. It was like I was frozen in time, like I wasn't even there. As my sister approached she said I had the strangest look on my face, a look of fascination and fear.

The comings and goings of the free world was something I hadn't witnessed for years. I knew guys who returned to prison of their own free will after purposely violating their parole because they could not take the real world. They were institutionalized. Having been told what to do and when to do it for so many years, they couldn't make decisions for themselves. We heard stories of trips to the grocery store that would leave a grown man completely overwhelmed by the choices in, for example, cereal only to realize that he had been standing in the aisle for an hour without making a decision. It is an amazing feeling to fear a thing like Cocoa Puffs. Was this going to happen to me? I had no idea what to expect.

Once again, I made a decision to embrace change and slowly things started to get a little less scary. My friends and family were there to give me support and I was able to visit a cereal aisle incident free. Then it hit me. I was relearning a lesson. Once again, I was standing at the gate of change, looking at my past and envisioning a future as a better man with a better life. But, until I decided to embrace the change by stepping through the gate to see what was ahead of me, there could be nothing for me but fear of the unknown.

Freedom was an awesome thing and it was meant to be a little scary to me. I had to relearn freedom from the standpoint of a sober, law-abiding citizen. I had to have it revealed to me in shocking clarity so that I would know that every moment I spent as a free man had amazing things in store for me. Becoming educated and surviving prison was only a short part of my path. Once I got out, I found that there would always be another challenge, another obstacle to overcome, another lesson to learn. I found that I was better than I had been, but I was still not the best I could be. This will always be true.

That is the warning in this chapter. You must learn to love the path to becoming the person you want to be, because it does not end. When you have finished the goal you set for yourself, at the beginning of this book, you will have a choice to make between continuing on the path or slipping back into dead time. In life, I will meet Janus again and again because as soon as I accomplish one goal, another must replace it. And, each time I meet him another test is passed and another lesson is learned. Dead time is no longer good enough for me nor will it be good enough for you.

◆◆◆

Not all of the gates I pass are huge and imposing and neither will yours be, but those are sometimes the challenges that can hold the greatest lessons.

I discovered I could not get auto insurance because I didn't have an insurance record for three years prior. Where I live, under state law, if you can't show proof of insurance for the prior three years it is illegal for the insurance companies to issue you a policy. This was intended to catch people who'd been driving without insurance, but left no loophole for someone such as myself who didn't need to carry insurance for prior years. Phone calls, letter writing and appealing my situation seemed to make no difference to anyone I contacted, and I was finally forced into informing an insurance company that the place I resided for the past three years did not require drivers to carry insurance. From that, I learned that there actually are still people in the world who prefer to think the best of you rather than the worst. I never said where I had been, but they were happy to assume that I had been in a foreign country. I'm sure that prison never crossed their minds. After years in the detention system, it was nice to finally be given the benefit of the doubt rather than the nightstick of unfounded assumption.

Upon obtaining insurance I tried to secure a driver's license, but was told because of a ten year old violation in another state, I would have to resolve that issue before my residing state would issue a license. Hence another six weeks of red tape and paperwork being passed from state to state before I was finally issued my drivers license. It forced me to remember that no matter who I became, I would always have to be accountable for my past.

I then attempted to rebuild my credit, but the bankers were shocked to see that not only did I lack a recent credit history, but also my credit report was completely blank, as if I had dropped off the face of the earth. I was informed that this was more damaging than having a bad credit report. I would have been better off showing a bankruptcy, a repossessed vehicle, anything. From that I learned that even a clean slate could present a challenge.

Of course the credit report is not the only place where there was a preference for a marred past. Inform someone that you spent the last several years incarcerated for armed bank robbery, and the reception is usually very cool. I learned quickly that it was better if people got to know me first, before I shared the details of my recent residence with them. Only then were they willing to look beyond the stigma at who I really was. The one exception to this is my current wife, the most nonjudgmental, caring, sweet, loving, honest and beautiful woman I have ever met. She knew my past before meeting me and was able to see beyond my history. She has taught me to look at the world with an open heart.

Easy times after my release? No. Worth working for and fighting through? Yes. That which is worthwhile in our life, which is really worthwhile, is never going to be easy. My dead time is over and every day, I choose a better life.

PART 3:
On Your Side

Four truths to take with you on your journey to a better life.

"We are bound by nothing except belief."
-Ernest Holmes

Chapter 9: Lock up Your Loved Ones

"All you need is love."

-John Lennon

When I discovered I was being released from prison five years earlier than I had expected, my family and I kept it a secret from my son, Eric. It just so happened that my release date was thirteen days before Christmas, so my parents quickly made arrangements for Eric to spend Christmas vacation with them in Phoenix. This didn't raise any red flags for Eric because he had been doing this every other year for this past seven years. On the day that my son flew into Phoenix Sky Harbor International Airport, my father, mother, brother, sister and I drove down to greet Eric. My mother, father and sister went to the gate Eric was scheduled to arrive at, and my brother and I stayed back four gates, I on one side of the hallway with a hat and sunglasses on, my brother on the other side with a video camera, taping the entire scene. As Eric got off the plane my parents and sister greeted him with hugs and kisses, and after exchanging pleasantries began heading in my direction. At this time, I stepped away from the wall and began walking towards them. As I approached them I stepped in front of the group and said, excuse me could someone please tell me what time it is? Out of the corner of my eye I could see my son's face, his mouth wide open and his eyes as big as saucers. Answering my question my mom said, "It's 7:30." "Thank you very much," I said and stepped around them, continuing on. Behind me I could hear my son saying, "That was my dad!" My father said, "That wasn't your Dad, Eric, you know where your Dad is." A second passed and my son said, "I'm telling you, Grandpa, that was my Dad. Go get him!" That, of course, was all I could take and I spun around, ran back to my son and spent the next five minutes hugging, kissing and crying. I definitely blew the little guy out of the water, and that was the first time in his entire life he had ever been rendered speechless.

◆◆◆

Family and loved ones, there is absolutely nothing more important. This bears repeating. There is absolutely nothing more important in our lives than the people we love and those who love us. I am in particular talking about the people in our everyday life, the people we oftentimes take for granted, the ones that we assume will always be there, the ones who we peck on the cheek as we walk in the door after a long day, only to then plop our butts on the coach. The people who get that same gesture as we leave the next morning. The people who we assume are always going to be a part of our life.

I'm here to tell you, they are not always going to be a part of our lives and they are not always going to be there. I didn't realize how important these people were in my life until they were taken away from me.

When we played this trick on my son, we were just trying to have a little good-natured fun, but what he gave me was yet another lesson in life – Be vigilant in your love. My son has played second fiddle to drugs in his father's eyes, he has been through high security prison searches, had to fend off countless attacks of ridicule for his father, and, when we played the trick on him in the airport, was willing to argue with those he trusted – his own grandparents – to be vigilant in his love for his father. It is amazing what you can learn from a child.

It is not *what* we have in our lives but *who*, and we all need to ask ourselves if we are spending the *least* time with what's *most* important. Let these people know you love them and let them know often. Make them feel special every day. Don't wait one more day lest it is too late. Regrets later are mistakes made today. Please don't ever take these people for granted.

I am fortunate enough to be surrounded by a family of people who, through trials and tribulations, have been vigilant in their love. When I was on drugs, they tried to intervene. When I lost touch, they didn't lose hope. When I was branded society's outcast, they hugged me tightest. When they were taken away from me, I finally knew their worth.

Let these people know you love them and let them know often. Let them know how special they are every day. Watch your kids and fight to protect them no matter how much they rebel against it. Pick up the phone and call your parents, or better yet, visit them, they will not always be there for you. Hug your loved ones close and be true to your commitments and you will have that love reflected back to you. Lock up your loved ones so that you will never have to regret the things that were not said or the love not given. They will be your cheerleaders, your confidants, and your reality check. As you are there for them, they will be there for you. It will make a difference to them and it will make a difference in you.

Chapter 10: Do Time, Don't Let It Do You

"We all have the same amount of time. You have the same amount of time as the average billionaire. It's not how much time you have, it's how you use the time you have."
-Larry Winget

To realize the value of one year, ask the student who has failed his final exam

To realize the value of one month, ask the mother who has given birth to a premature baby.

To realize the value of one week, ask the editor of a weekly newspaper.

To realize the value of one day, ask the daily wage laborer with ten kids to feed.

To realize the value of one hour, ask the lovers who are waiting to meet.

To realize the value of one minute, ask the person who has missed the plane.

To realize the value of one second, ask the person who has survived an accident.

To realize the value of a millisecond, ask the person who has won a silver medal in the Olympics.

To realize the value of time, in any increment, ask the person who spent 12.5 years as a slave to drugs, followed by 7.5 years as an incarcerated felon.

Time is our most valuable commodity bar none. It is, hands down, the most precious thing we have, yet it is the one thing with which we are most often wasteful. You can't recycle it, regain it, rejuvenate it, rediscover it, or reuse it. Once it's gone, it's gone. Now, I'm not saying we shouldn't have relaxation time, hobby time, lay on the couch and read a book time, or sit in the sun and do absolutely nothing time. It's all about balance in our lives. What I'm saying is that you need to respect and cherish it as you would any precious gift and realize that every moment that you are not using it to live the life you deserve is dead time wasted.

There was a guy that I knew in prison named Charlie Dotson. Charlie was a good guy as far as a con goes – minded his own business, very respectful of others, never got in anybody's way, centerfielder on my softball team. Charlie and I worked in UNICOR, Federal Prison Industries, a manufacturing facility within the institution. We built furniture. I worked upstairs in the business office. Charlie worked downstairs on the production floor assembling furniture. One day I walked over to the copier and as my copy was running I looked out the big plate glass window in front of me, and on the concrete floor below lay my friend Charlie Dotson, a six-foot pool of blood surrounding his head. Standing over Charlie was another inmate with a four-foot oak table leg that he had used to bash in Charlie's head. Judging by the pool of blood, by the time I saw him, Charlie had been dead for some time. Thirty to forty other inmates stood in a circle around his limp body having witnessed the whole thing. Nobody had lifted a hand to stop what they were seeing. Nobody called a guard. Everyone just walked away knowing that they could be in Charlie's place the next day, the next hour, the next minute.

Charlie lost his life that day because of a 69¢ writing pen. The assailant accused Charlie of walking by his workstation, picking up his 69¢ pen, thus disrespecting him and giving him the right to take Charlie's life. Charlie had a wife of ten years, an eight-year-old daughter, and six weeks left on a six-year prison sentence. In that instant it was all snatched away. A father was lost, a widow was made, and a future vanished into thin air, all over 69¢ pen.

I've often wondered what unfinished business Charlie had. After all, there were only six short weeks left before the world would be open to him again. Was he waiting for the right moment to tell his wife and daughter how much they really meant to him? Did he look forward to the day, six weeks down the road, that he would be able to start rebuilding those relationships? Was he waiting for the best time, place and circumstances? If he was, he may have missed his opportunity altogether.

It gives you something to think about. We've all heard the saying, "Live every day as if it is your last," but how many of us follow it? How many of us, if hit by a bus tomorrow, could say that we had done everything in our power to live the lives we wanted? Would we go to our graves knowing that we had found that career, climbed that mountain, made time for the kids, or died trying? Or would we, instead, make a lot of excuses for why it had never been the perfect time to start?

Living the life that you deserve takes diligence. It takes a flat out rejection of dead time. It takes a plan.

Personally, I have my own time management tool that keeps me on the path to being the man I want to be. It's not a planner or PDA. I simply have goals. It's that easy. I have both short and long-term goals that revolve around every facet of my life, not just my career. Goals for my relationships, my health, vacations, experiences, purchases, everything. Throughout the day, just by habit I ask myself, "Is what you're doing right now, getting you any closer to those goals?" If the answer is no, I change what I'm doing. It's that simple. I never have to refill my pages. I never run out of a battery. My goals are with me twenty-four-seven, emblazoned on the chalkboard of my mind with great big priority exclamation marks next to them. I don't have to write them down. They're too important. How could I forget them? Writing something down means that you need a reminder, and needing a reminder means that you are not actively living your life to attain your goals, to be the person you want to be.

I look back now at all of the wasted years, from my teens where drugs became the central focal point of my existence, and I look at the days I spent in prison becoming the person that I am today. If I had always known the value of time, what could I have accomplished? If I don't respect that time now, what will I miss?

Of course you will have to make your own goals and priorities, but I want to spend a couple of moments on the tools that you will need to reach them. Before you start envisioning your new Ferrari or house in the hills, make your first goals to yourself. Like I said, time is precious. Spend it on the things that will give you the skills to make all of your other goals a reality – your mind, body, and soul.

When I talk about improving your mind, I do not necessarily mean academics, although that direction would certainly foot the bill. I am talking about anything that stimulates you intellectually, expands your knowledge base, or offers a challenge between the ears. Read a book. Write a book. Paint a picture. Take a cooking class. Research a topic you know nothing about. Build a model airplane using step-by-step instructions. Learn a new trade.

Your activity may correlate to an overall goal that you are working towards at the time, or it may just be an exercise to keep the brain agile for when you really need it. What's important here is that we charter new waters, challenge the mind, and explore new possibilities. If not stimulated the mind becomes stale, shuts down to the change around it, and in actuality, serves as a hindrance to our advancement and success. It is important to keep your mind sharp to prevent that from happening. They say idle hands are the devil's playground. I say an idle mind is an invitation for dead time.

With the engine now running, it's time to assure that the body and frame are equally up for the task. Your current goals may have nothing to do with your physiology, but your overall health affects every part of your life. You don't need hours of justification or the depths of self-loathing to inspire you. Just remember, better health makes life easier. It will keep you going when you have to work harder, it will give you the ability to handle stress better, and it will open up new possibilities for enjoying life. As an added benefit, it will get you up those stairs faster.

For me it's jogging and weight lifting. For you it could be Yoga, climbing stairs, walking the dog, swimming, basketball, tennis, anything that leads to improving our physical well-being. It is not important what it is, but that we do it as a regular part of our schedule. You have to make it a habit. That is the key! I could no more miss my workout than I could miss breakfast or brushing my teeth before bed each evening. It is part of my daily routine and will become part of yours if given the chance to become a habit, a normal occurrence that requires no thought, just an assumed part of the day. Once it becomes second nature, you won't even have to talk yourself into it. It will just be another valued part of your day. I do my best thinking, come up with my best ideas while jogging. Some may find jogging to be boring, and prefer competitive sports. I have friends who enjoy the peacefulness of yoga. My parents like the intimacy of holding hands and walking each evening. The venue does not matter, only that we make a choice.

You may feel like you are already in good physical condition, but dead time can find you here as well. Challenge yourself. Start somewhere, but as an activity becomes boring or easy, move onto something that pushes your limitations, teaches you new balance, or improves flexibility. Just as with the mind, the body is most easily improved when challenged. Try different activities, those you thought you may never be interested in or that you would be unable to do. Later, when it comes time to meet an important deadline, win a race, or play with the grandkids, you will be ready.

While getting the mind and the body on the same page, don't forget your soul. I am not going to expound upon religious dogma here. That is an individual choice and I will leave you to it. My advice is simply that you continually strive to find your way to your own peace. This may happen through organized religion, meditation, counseling, volunteerism, or spending the day recognizing the little blessings that surround you. Your soul is your guide, your lodestone to taking the right path to becoming the person you want to be. You cannot enjoy a new job if your soul is ill at ease over the way you obtained it. You will not take pleasure in your new physique if you abused yourself to mold it. You will not cherish your success if you selfishly hoard it. In short, you cannot have triumphs of the mind and body without your soul, so nurture it.

Think of these three areas of improvement as the necessities that you will want to have in your backpack as you travel your path. Once you have these three areas of your life finely tuned and in perpetual motion, you will find that your goals come more and more easily and the path seems clearer than ever. You will be alert, spry and at peace and those are three very good things when you are on a journey. If you invest in yourself in these three areas, the rest of your goals will seem suddenly attainable and you will know the satisfaction of never feeling remorse at the passage of time.

Chapter 11: Take the Key Away
From the Guard

"You are what you are and where you are because of what has gone into your mind, and you can change what you are and where you are by changing what goes into your mind."
-Zig Ziglar

What goes around comes around, Divine Intervention, Karma, Fate – people have been naming forces behind the paths that we take for millennia. Like I said before, I am not here to argue religious dogma, but I do want to share some truths that I have gleaned from my life's experiences. They are based in faith. The faith that every person has a purpose and a potential that is waiting to be fulfilled and we are rewarded or schooled based on the choices that we make along that path.

Think about all of the things that have happened in your life that make up who you are today. Have you ever had anything go so exactly right that you could only explain it as luck? Did you take advantage of the luck in the best way possible, or did you waste it? Have you ever had something devastating happen to you that has made you ask "Why me?" Did you find an answer to that question? Did you try?

There are some children's books that are called "Choose Your Own Adventure." They take the reader along a plot line and then, at a key point, ask them to make a crucial decision about what they would do. Once the reader makes the decision, they turn to the page corresponding to that decision and learn their fate. That is kind of how I feel about life. There are numerous outcomes that are already written, but it is up to us to make the right choices.

Let's give it a shot.

You're Troy Evans.

You move to a new town and have the choice of toughing it out until you can make new friends on the sports teams and in school, or you start doing bad things to make friends with the kids most available to you even though you know it is wrong. You chose the bad kids, turn to that page of the book and discover, oh bad luck, you will be an addict for most of your life.

You get married and have a kid. Do you choose to use your family's interventions to clean up your act and be a good husband and father or do you choose drugs? Sorry, the drugs page says that your wife leaves you and takes your son with her.

Do you get sober or rob banks to feed a habit. You choose to rob several banks in the hopes of either getting another fix or getting killed. Bad luck again, you're sent to jail to spend several years with yourself, thinking of every wrong that you've ever perpetrated against your family.

But here is where it gets interesting. The plot line can change as soon as you start making good decisions.

Once in jail, you choose sobriety over drugs, and gain clarity and a visit from your son who tells you that there is still hope.

You choose to fight to educate yourself rather than serving dead time, and a scholarship fund from the National Speakers Association that was never intended for a person like you is opened up to you.

You choose death over asking your family to smuggle drugs into the prison for you, and the guards come in at just the right moment.

When all of your hard work is snatched away from you, you choose to start over rather than return to drugs and the life you fought your way out of, and you are told that you get to go home.

And my favorite, you choose a life of speaking to make a difference in other people's lives and, through the man who volunteers to be your mentor, you are introduced to the kind, beautiful, accepting woman whom you make your wife.

There is just too much coincidence. The more I think about it and the more I talk to others about their experiences, the more I am convinced that when you are choosing the bad path, you can get only bad, when choosing the good path, good things are returned to you tenfold. How many sayings do we have about this exact same thing? You reap what you sew... What goes around comes around...

Of course, it is important that you keep your eyes open because the punishments do not always happen right away and the good things are not always delivered in the best packages, but once you start making the right decisions, even the past returning to haunt you can be turned into a blessing. I received one such lesson a relatively short time after being released from prison.

My first indication that something was wrong came as I opened up the front door upon returning home from the office. The contents of our hallway closet completely littered the walkway in front of me. Upon entering the other rooms in the house I discovered each room had every single drawer and cabinet pulled out and upturned. We had been burglarized. On that day, every single item of value belonging to me and my wife of two months was taken. TV, VCR, stereo, computer, printer, fax, silver settings handed down to my wife from her grandmother, and all of my wife's jewelry, including things that were handed down from her grandparents and her parents. Things that could never be replaced. Every single thing of value that we owned was gone. In addition to the monetary loss, every single room in our home was ransacked, and it would be days before our home resembled anything close to the home we knew. Was I angry? I was very angry. Did I want revenge? Of course I wanted revenge, I wanted more than anything to get my hands on those who violated me, who had entered my space, who had taken from me.

Two days later while sitting at my desk filling out insurance forms and compiling the list of what had been taken, I got to thinking about why it was that this happened to me. And it slowly became apparent to me. I had never been on this end. I had never been the one who had been violated, victimized or stolen from. You see it had always been me who had been the taker, me the thief, me the one who had victimized people. I never knew what it felt like to be the victim, to be violated and to feel taken advantage of. As I thought about this over the next several days I came to the conclusion that, like every other significant thing that had happened in my life, this too had a reason.

I needed to feel this end of the equation. This was the final piece in the puzzle that brought me full circle from robber to victim. It emphasized the importance of my transformation. Slowly, I felt my anger dissipate and a peace replaced it. I had to feel that pain to know in my heart that I would never cause anyone that kind of suffering again.

They say that hindsight is 20/20, but I think that if it is closely regarded, it can be used to create incredible foresight. Looking back, I feel as though everything that has ever happened to me has happened for a reason. I live my life today based on that. Call it fate, call it the hand of God, call it Karma or Kismet. Call it whatever you want, but take a good look at the lesson that is true in all. Good works produce rewards. If you put good out to the universe, good works, good choices, good vibes, whatever you want to call it, it will be returned to you. Have faith in that and you will not get lost.

Chapter 12: The Prosecution of Our Past

"It's not what you are that holds you back, it's what you think you're not."
-Denis Waitley

It is not important how we come to the events in our life. What is important is how we deal with those events. Or, as I like to call this chapter, "There is no such thing as a good excuse."

In this book, I have shared tales with you from my darkest hours and stories of my scholarships, my 4.0 GPA, and my placement on the Deans and President's list. I did not share them with you in order to brag. I told them to you with the hope that it would become clear that absolutely anything could be accomplished out here in the free world. If I can accomplish what I did within the harsh and violent confines of the federal prison, you can accomplish absolutely anything you want with all of the resources at your disposal.

In chapter one, I talked about the little voice. The one that tells you why you can't accomplish your goals. I talked about using hope to banish that voice, but now I'm going to give you the final blow just in case you find that it is still hanging around every now and again. Are you ready? This is going to be pretty profound. Here it is.

That voice is a liar.

Listen to it for a second... "You can't afford college." Liar! "You're too old to change your life." Liar! "You hit your wife because she deserves it." Liar! "You can't quit because your addiction is more potent than other people's." Liar!

How do I know that the voice is lying? Because those are all excuses and when it comes to what is best for you, there is no such thing as a good excuse. Can't afford college? Bull, I did it from prison. Too old? I've known older. She deserves to be beat? No one deserves that. You suffer from a super potent, mega addiction? Mine made me stick a gun in the faces of innocent people and rob banks. I kicked it.

I don't care what your background is, I don't care how you were raised, I don't care what ethnic group or creed you belong to, and I don't care what kind of bumps, bruises, potholes or obstacles life has thrown your way. You can accomplish absolutely anything you want to accomplish if you want it bad enough. Throw away the excuses and you will be set free to be the person you want to be. Cling to them and you will always fail for having never tried.

I heard this story while I was in prison and I want to share it with you. It's a story about two brothers who come from the very same event, yet have very different outcomes.

From Australia comes a story of two brothers caught stealing sheep. The penalty for the crime was fierce. A brand of the letters "ST" was seared into each one's forehead, forever marking them as "Sheep Thieves."

For one brother the humiliation was overwhelming. Sneaking from town to town, he became crafty and cruel. Yet he could never get away from himself, and finally he died under suspicious circumstances after years of inner torment.

The other brother decided he had to face this crisis or be destroyed by. He chose to earn back his self-respect. He began each day with the question "What can I do today to earn back my self respect?"

As years unfolded, people began to trust him, and his past crime became a forgotten story on old newsprint. As he aged, he became a respected leader of the community, a friend of those who struggled, and an example of courage for the young.

Many years later a visitor came to town. He was surprised when he saw an old man shuffling past a store with the letters "ST" branded on his forehead. So he asked the clerk, "Who's that man? What's that all about?" The clerk said, "He used to be the mayor here. There was some story about how he got those scars on his forehead, but I can't remember what it was. I think it has to do with him being a saint."

Drop the excuses. It is time for you to succeed.

"I may not be the man I want to be;
I may not be the man I ought to be;
I may not be the man I could be;
I may not be the man I can be;
but praise God, I'm not the man I once was."
                              -Martin Luther King Jr.

About the Author

Troy Evans is a professional speaker and author who resides in Phoenix, Arizona with his wife Pam and his dog Archibald. Troy travels the country delivering keynote presentations, and since his release from prison has taken the corporate and association platforms by storm. Overcoming adversity, adapting to change and pushing yourself to realize your full potential.

Do you know a group that would benefit from hearing Troy's message? For information on booking Troy, or other available products, please contact:

The Evans Group
3104 E. Camelback Road, #436
Phoenix, AZ 85016
602-265-6855
Fax: 602-285-1474
troy@troyevans.com
www.troyevans.com